I0169661

Translations of Favorite German and English Poems

Fritz VonderHeiden

Translations of Favorite German and English Poems

Copyright © 2013 by Frederick VonderHeiden
Cover copyright © 2013 by Sunbury Press, Inc.
Cover image "Bad Wimpfen" by Lawrence von Knorr

SCOND SUNBURY PRESS EDITION
Printed in the United States of America
November 2013

Trade paperback ISBN: 978-1-62006-221-0

Published by:
Sunbury Press
Mechanicsburg, PA
www.sunburypress.com

Mechanicsburg, Pennsylvania   USA

Table of Contents

GERMAN

ENGLISH

German
to
English

Erlkönig
von
Johann Wolfgang von Goethe

Wer reitet so spät durch Nacht und Wind?
Es ist der Vater mit seinem Kind;
Er hat den Knaben wohl in dem Arm,
Er faßt ihn sicher, er hält ihn warm.

"Mein Sohn, was birgst du so bang dein Gesicht?" –
"Siehst, Vater, du den Erlkönig nicht?
Den Erlenkönig mit Kron und Schweif?" –
"Mein Sohn, es ist ein Nebelstreif."

"Du liebes Kind, komm, geh mit mir!
Gar schöne Spiele spiel' ich mit dir;
Manch' bunte Blumen sind an dem Strand,
Meine Mutter hat manch gülden Gewand." –

"Mein Vater, mein Vater, und hörest du nicht,
Was Erlenkönig mir leise verspricht?" –
"Sei ruhig, bleibe ruhig, mein Kind;
In dürren Blättern säuselt der Wind." –

"Willst, feiner Knabe, du mit mir gehen?
Meine Töchter sollen dich warten schön;
Meine Töchter führen den nächtlichen Reihn,
Und wiegen und tanzen und singen dich ein." –

"Mein Vater, mein Vater, und siehst du nicht dort
Erlkönigs Töchter am düstern Ort?" –
"Mein Sohn, mein Sohn, ich seh es genau:
Es scheinen die alten Weiden so grau. –"

"Ich liebe dich, mich reizt deine schöne Gestalt;
Und bist du nicht willig, so brauch ich Gewalt." –
"Mein Vater, mein Vater, jetzt faßt er mich an!
Erlkönig hat mir ein Leids getan!" –

Dem Vater grauset's, er reitet geschwind,
Er hält in Armen das ächzende Kind,
Erreicht den Hof mit Müh' und Not;
In seinen Armen das Kind war tot.

The Elf King
by
Johann Wolfgang von Goethe

Who is it that's riding so late in the night?
A father - who's holding his son very tight;
He keeps the boy close to his own sturdy form,
To make very sure that he's sheltered and warm.

What is it, my son, that frightens you so?
The Elf King, Father, - he's there, don't you know?
He's wearing a crown, and a swallowtail too -
My son, it is nothing but fog and some dew.

"Dear boy, let us play a few make-believe games,
Like looking for flowers with colorful names,
The bloom on the beaches of by-the-sea towns,
Or finding some gold in your grandmother's gowns."

O Father, my Father, but didn't you hear,
What Elf King whispered just now in my ear?
Be peaceful, my child, there has nothing been said;
It's only the wind in the leaves overhead.

"Dear boy, we'll get home just as soon as we can,
Your sisters are waiting according to plan,
To welcome you home and their promises keep,
To dance you and sing you and rock you to sleep."

O Father, my Father, but surely you see,
The Elf King's daughters out there in the lea.
- My son, I can see, - what you point to is clear;
It's only some withered old willows you fear.

I love you, dear fellow, and only too well,
But if you won't listen I'll have to compel -
O Father, my Father, he's grabbing my arm!
The terrible Elf King has done me a harm!

Now fearful, the father soon quickens his pace,
The whimpering youngster still in his embrace;
When finally he reaches the grounds of his stead,
The woebegone boy at his bosom was dead.

Ein Traum
von
Friedrich von Schiller

Ein Traum, ein Traum ist unser Leben
Auf Erden hier.
Wie Schatten auf den Wogen schweben
Und schwinden wir.
Wir messen unsre träge' Tritte
Nach Raum und Zeit.
Und sind, und wissen's nicht, in Mitte
Der Ewigkeit.

A Dream
by
Friedrich von Schiller

This life of ours is like, so like a dream,
On this planet here.
We flutter like the shadows on a stream,
Then disappear.
By time and space we gauge our earthly treks,
With goodly certainty,
And are, on which no one of us reflects,
Amidst eternity.

Barbarossa
von
Friedrich Rückert

Der alte Barbarossa,
Der Kaiser Friederich,
Im unterird'schen Schlosse
Hält er verzaubert sich.

Er ist niemals gestorben,
Er lebt darin noch jetzt;
Er hat im Schloß verborgen
Zum Schlaf sich hingesetzt.

Er hat hinab genommen
Des Reiches Herrlichkeit
Und wird einst wiederkommen
Mir ihr zu seiner Zeit.

Der Stuhl ist elfenbeinern,
Darauf der Kaiser sitzt;
Der Tisch ist marmelsteinern,
Worauf sein Haupt er stützt.

Sein Bart ist nicht von Flachse,
Er ist von Feuersglut,
Ist durch den Tisch gewachsen,
Worauf sein Haupt ausruht.

Er nickt als wie im Traume,
Sein Aug' halb offen zwinkt,
Und je nach langem Raume
Er einem Knaben winkt.

Er spricht im Schlaf zum Knaben:
Geh hin vor's Schloß, o Zwerg,
Und sieh, ob noch die Raben
Herfliegen um den Berg.

Und wenn die alten Raben
Noch fliegen immerdar,
So muß ich auch noch schlafen,
Verzaubert hundert Jahr.

Barbarossa
by
Friedrich Rückert

Inside a castle, underground,
Old Barbarrosa sits;
There by his own dark magic bound,-
The Redbeard Kaiser Fritz.

He never really died, you see,
He lives there to this day;
He hid down there where he'd be free,
To sleep the years away.

He took his kingdom's glory there,
But someday will return,
And bring it back with stately care,
That we its might may learn.

He sits upon an ivory chair,
And rests his noble head,
Upon a marble table there,
That serves him as its bed.

His beard, not flaxen, - flame-like grown,
Its fiery embers glow;
It's burnt right through the marbled stone,
And reached the floor below.

A sudden nod! - like in a dream,
A blink from half-closed eye;
And soon he beckons, it would seem,
A boy-sized man nearby.

Still half asleep, he tells the man,
To go outside and see,
If ravens still fly 'round the land,
And o'er the mountain be.

"O Dwarf," he says, "if they still fly,
I must stay in this keep,
Until a hundred years go by
And break this magic sleep."

Die Lorelei
von
Heinrich Heine

Ich weiß nicht, was soll es bedeuten,
Daß ich so traurig bin,
Ein Märchen aus uralten Zeiten,
Das kommt mir nicht aus dem Sinn.
Die Luft ist kühl und es dunkelt,
Und ruhig fließt der Rhein;
Der Gipfel des Berges funkelt,
Im Abendsonnenschein.

Die schönste Jungfrau sitzet
Dort oben wunderbar,
Ihr gold'nes Geschmeide blitzet,
Sie kämmt ihr goldenes Haar,
Sie kämmt es mit goldenem Kamme,
Und singt ein Lied dabei;
Das hat eine wundersame,
Gewalt'ge Melodei.

Den Schiffer im kleinen Schiffe,
Ergreift es mit wildem Weh;
Er schaut nicht die Felsenriffe,
Er schaut nur hinauf in die Höh'.
Ich glaube, die Wellen verschlingen
Am Ende Schiffer und Kahn,
Und das hat mit ihrem Singen,
Die Loreley getan.

The Lorelei
by
Heinrich Heine

What it could mean, I do not know,
Myself so sad to find;
A fable told from long ago,
That will not leave my mind.

The air is cool as dusk comes nigh,
The Rhine serenely flows;
A mountaintop still gleams on high,
Where evening sunlight shows.

A woman sits up on this height,
Resplendent, young and fair;
Her golden jewels catch the light;
She combs her golden hair

She combs it with a comb of gold,
And sings a song of love,
With melody so bright and bold,
It drifts down from above.

A boatman in a skiff comes by,
And is enchanted so,
He only sees the maid on high,
And not the reefs below.

His boat and he soon disappear,
Their passage gone awry;
Devoured by the waves, I fear,
And of the song of Lorelei.

Du Bist Wie Eine Blume
von
Heinrich Heine

Du bist wie eine Blume,
So hold und schön und rein;
Ich schau' dich an und Wehmut
Schleicht mir ins Herz hinein.

Mir ist, als ob ich die Hände
Aufs Haupt dir liegen sollt',
Betend, daß Gott dich erhalte
So rein und schön und hold.

You're Lovely Like a Flower
by
Heinrich Heine

You're lovely like a flower,
So fine and pure and fair;
I look at you and yearnings
Bestir my heart to care.

It seems, upon your head, I should
Lay both of these hands of mine,
And pray that you be kept by God,
So fair and pure and fine.

English
to
German

Trees
by
Joyce Kilmer

I THINK that I shall never see
A poem lovely as a tree.

A tree whose hungry mouth is prest
Against the earth's sweet flowing breast;

A tree that looks at God all day,
And lifts her leafy arms to pray;

A tree that may in Summer wear
A nest of robins in her hair;

Upon whose bosom snow has lain;
Who intimately lives with rain.

Poems are made by fools like me,
But only God can make a tree.

Bäume
von
Joyce Kilmer

Nie habe ich auf ein Gedicht,
so herrlich wie ein Baum geblickt.

Ein Baum mit Munde angedrückt,
der süßen Brust des Erdens dicht.

Ein Baum, der Gott ansehend lebt,
belaubte Arme betend hebt.

Ein Baum, der oft im Sommer trägt,
ein Vogelnest im Haar gelegt.

Sein Busen oft mit Schnee bedeckt,
und lebt vertraut mit Regen recht.

Gedichte sind von Narr'n erdacht;
Nur Gott ist es, der Bäume macht.

Sea-Fever
by
John Masefield

I must go down to the seas again, to the lonely
sea and the sky,
And all I ask is a tall ship and a star to steer
her by,
And the wheel's kick and the wind's song and
the white sail's shaking,
And a grey mist on the sea's face, and a grey
dawn breaking.

I must go down to the seas again, for the call
of the running tide
Is a wild call and a clear call that may not be
denied;
And all I ask is a windy day with the white
clouds flying,
And the flung spray and the blown spume, and
the sea-gulls crying.

I must go down to the seas again, to the
vagrant gypsy life,
To the gull's way and the whale's way, where
the wind's like a whetted knife;
And all I ask is a merry yarn from a laughing
fellow-rover,
And quiet sleep and a sweet dream when the
long trick's over.

Seefieber
von
John Masefield

Wieder muß ich an die Seen, den Himmel und
die öde See erleben,
Ich brauche nur ein Segelschiff, und einen
Stern, den rechten Kurs zu geben;
Ich möchte auch den Windgesang und
Steuerruck, und Flattern weißer Segel,
Den grauen Tagesanbruch und die tiefe graue
Nebel.

Wieder muß ich an die Seen, - der Ruf von
Tidefluß,
Ist klar und wild, - ein Mächtiger, dem man
gehorchen muß;
Ich bitte nur um starken Wind, und Wolken
hoch und weiß,
Und dichten Gischt und reifen Schaum, und
Schrei von Möwen dreist.

Wieder muß ich an die Seen, - zigeunerisch als
Meeresstreicher leben,
Wie Walfische und Möwen, - wo Winde, wie ein
Messer, Stich erregen;
Ich brauche nur ein frisches Garn, mit Lachen
von 'nem Mitschiffsmann,
Und sanften Schlaf mit süßem Traum, - wenn
langes Reisen enden kann.

21

Believe Me If All Those
Endearing Young Charms
by
Thomas Moore

Believe me, if all those endearing young charms,
Which I gaze on so fondly today,
Were to change by tomorrow and fleet in my arms,
Like fairy wings fading away.

Thou wouldst still be adored, as this moment thou art,
Let thy loveliness fade as it will;
And around the dear ruin each wish of my heart
Would entwine itself verdantly still.

It is not while beauty and youth are thine own,
And thy cheeks unprofaned by a tear,
That the fervor and faith of a soul can be known,
To which time will but make thee more dear.

No, the heart that has truly loved never forgets,
But as truly loves on to the close:
As the sunflower turns on her god when he sets
The same look which she turned when he rose.

Glaub' Es Mir Wenn
Deine Zärtliche' Charme
von
Thomas Moore

Glaub' es mir wenn deine zärtliche Charme,
Charme der Jugend worauf jetzt ich starre,
Morgen verändert, geschwunden mir wären,
Würde ich trotzdem dich weiter verehren.

Möchte dein' Schönheit sich willig vermindern,
Würde das wahrlich mein' Liebe nicht hindern;
Jeder Begehr meines Herzens gewunden,
Um deine alte Gestalt fest gebunden.

Nicht als du Jugend und Schönheit besitzt,
Und Haut auf den Wangen noch tränenlos ist,
Kann jemand die Treue 'ner Seele erfahren, Eher
wenn wirst du mir lieber nach Jahren!

Ein Herz welches wahrlich liebt, nimmer vergisst,
Und liebt aber weiter solange du bist;
Wie Blumen der Sonne an ihren Gott sehen,
Beim Untergang so wie am Aufgang sich drehend!

Barbara Frietchie
by
John Greenleaf Whittier

Up from the meadows rich with corn,
Clear in the cool September morn,

The clustered spires of Frederick stand
Green-walled by the hills of Maryland.

Round about them orchards sweep,
Apple- and peach-tree fruited deep,

Fair as the garden of the Lord
To the eyes of the famished rebel horde,

On that pleasant morn of the early fall
When Lee marched over the mountain wall,—

Over the mountains winding down,
Horse and foot, into Frederick town.

Forty flags with their silver stars,
Forty flags with their crimson bars,

Flapped in the morning wind: the sun
Of noon looked down, and saw not one.

Up rose old Barbara Frietchie then,
Bowed with her fourscore years and ten;

Bravest of all in Frederick town,
She took up the flag the men hauled down;

In her attic window the staff she set,
To show that one heart was loyal yet.

Up the street came the rebel tread,
Stonewall Jackson riding ahead.

Under his slouched hat left and right
He glanced: the old flag met his sight.

"Halt!"— the dust-brown ranks stood fast.
"Fire!"— out blazed the rifle-blast.

It shivered the window, pane and sash;
It rent the banner with seam and gash.

Quick, as it fell, from the broken staff
Dame Barbara snatched the silken scarf;

She leaned far out on the window-sill,
And shook it forth with a royal will.

"Shoot, if you must, this old gray head,
But spare your country's flag," she said.

A shade of sadness, a blush of shame,
Over the face of the leader came;

The nobler nature within him stirred
To life at that woman's deed and word:

"Who touches a hair of yon gray head
Dies like a dog! March on!" he said.

All day long through Frederick street
Sounded the tread of marching feet:

All day long that free flag tost
Over the heads of the rebel host.

Ever its torn folds rose and fell
On the loyal winds that loved it well;

And through the hill-gaps sunset light
Shone over it with a warm good-night.

Barbara Frietchie's work is o'er,
And the Rebel rides on his raids no more.

Honor to her! and let a tear
Fall, for her sake, on Stonewall's bier.

Over Barbara Frietchie's grave
Flag of Freedom and Union, wave!

Peace and order and beauty draw
Round thy symbol of light and law;

And ever the stars above look down
On thy stars below in Frederick town!

Barbara Frietchie
von
John Greenleaf Whittier

Oben von grünen mit Mais reichen Wiesen,
Klar in den kühleren Frühmorgenbrisen,
Stehen die Fred'ricker Türme beisammen,
Umgeben mit Hügeln als erdgrünem Rahmen.

Und drum reichen Obstgärten überall weit,
Bäume mit Äpfeln und Pfirsichen reich.
So schön wie der biblische Garten es war,
Den Augen der hungrigen Rebellenschar.

Am Morgen im Herbste 'was früh in dem Krieg,
Als Lee mit Soldaten den Berg überstieg;
Berge herüber und unten sie kamen,
'ne Schlange von Pferden und Männern zusammen.

Mit vierzig Fahnen Fred'rick erreichend,
Kamen sie kühn mit Sternen und Streifen.
Hochrote Streifen und silberne Sterne, Flatternde
Zeichen der Rebellenheere.

Die vierzig Fahnen im Morgenwind wehend; Die
Mittagssonne doch gar keine sehend.
Dann tratt alte Barbara auf,
Krumm von neunzigjährigem Lauf;

Die tapferste Bürger in Frederick Stadt,
Gestrichene Flagge besorgte sie flott.
Im Dachbodenfenster sie stellte den Stab,
Als Zeichen dass <u>ein</u> Herz die Treue noch hab'.

27

Die Strasse entlang kam der Rebellenschritt,
Jackson voraus, - und trefflich er ritt.
Er blickte rechts, und links darauf, von unterm
schrägen Hut,
Erblickte bald die Flagge denn sien Augenlicht war
gut.

Stand jeder Mann still, als laut rief er "Halt! --
Feuer!" befahl, und Schiessgewehr' knallt'.
Sie brachen des Fensters die Scheiben und
Rahmen;
Sie rissen mit Löchern und Schnitten die Fahne.

Als schnell stürzte diese vom Stabstücke nieder,
So schnell holte Barbara die Seidene wieder.
Oben zurück, sie lehnte sich weit vom Simse
heraus,
Und schüttelte dringend die Fahne und Faust.

"Schiesst dieses graue Haupt," sie sagte, "wenn ihr
dieses wollt,
Schont doch die Fahne ihres Landes, wie ihr eher
sollt."
Ein' Spur von Schwermut, und Röte der Schande,
Erschienen im Antlitz des führenden Mannes;

Als Jackson Barbaras Worte, ihren Wagemut
vernahm,
Entstand das ed'l're Wesen, das von Tiefe seiner
kam.
"Wer der Frau ein Haar verkrümmnt," er sagte
irritiert,
"infolgedessen wie ein Köter fertig ist krepiert! -
Vorwarts!"

Den ganzen Tag lang konnte jedermann hören,
Marschierende Füsse die Strassen verstören.
Den ganzen Tag durch, das verlässige Tuch
Flatterte über dem fremden Besuch.

Sein rissiger Stoff wogte auf und ab
Im treuen Winde, der Freude ihm gab.
Dann schien --durch die Hügel, des Abendlichts
Pracht,
Als wünschte es gütig der Fahne "Gut' Nacht."

Vorbei is die Barbara Frietchies Wehr,
Und Reiter der Rebellen streifen nicht mehr.
Lass unser Lob auf Frau Barbara hallen,
Auch eine Träne auf Stonewalls Grab fallen.

Über Frau Barbaras schlichtem Grabe,
Weh' die alleinige Freitheitsflagge!
Ziehen der Frieden und Ordnungsbegriff,
Um ihre Fahne des Rechtes und Lichts;

Sehen die Sterne des Himmels herab,
Ewig auf Bürger der Frederick Stadt!

The Last Rose of Summer
by
Thomas Moore

'Tis the last rose of summer,
Left blooming alone;
All her lovely companions
Are faded and gone;
No flower of her kindred,
No rosebud is nigh,
To reflect back her blushes,
Or give sigh for sigh.

I'll not leave thee, thou lone one!
To pine on the stem;
Since the lovely are sleeping,
Go, sleep thou with them.
Thus kindly I scatter,
Thy leaves o'er the bed,
Where thy mates of the garden
Lie scentless and dead.

So soon may I follow,
When friendships decay,
And from Love's shining circle
The gems drop away.
When true hearts lie withered,
And fond ones are flown,
Oh! who would inhabit
This bleak world alone?

Des Sommers Letzte Rose
von
Thomas Moore

Des Sommers letzte Rose,
Bleibt blühend ganz allein;
Die schönen Zeitgenossen sind
Geschwunden, bleich, und klein;
Nah gibt es keine Blume,
Noch Knopse ihrer Art,
Mit der sie das Erröten
Ihrer Blüten schätzen darf.

Ich wollte dich nicht lassen,
Bei dir am Stengel sehnen;
Geh also eben schlaffen,
Bei and'ren stillen Schönen.
Da streu' ich lieb ihr' Blätter
Ans Beet woran es liegt
Die Schwesterhaft des Gartens,
Nun duftlos - totbetrübt.

Bald folge ich dir irgendwann,
Wenn Freundschaft mir verfällt,
Geschmeide von der Krone
Des Liebenskreises fällt;
Wenn treue Herzen welken,
Und Freunde gehen ein,
Wer wollte noch bewohen,
Die öde Welt allein?

www.ingramcontent.com/pod-product-compliance
Lightning Source LLC
Chambersburg PA
CBHW031637040426
42452CB00007B/853